MW00927819

Other Books By Felix Harder

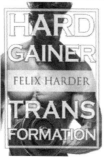  

Click On The Cover To Go To The Book

Introduction

Introduction

This book includes the 48 best gym exercises for building strength and gaining muscle. Most of these exercises are timeless and have been performed by bodybuilders for decades. They are proven to work and should be part of every workout routine.

Unfortunately, many beginners, and even some experienced trainees, don't use proper form. Oftentimes, they simply copy their friends at the gym, which can lead to injuries and long-term joint problems. To spare yourself such issues, you need to educate yourself on how to train correctly.

I divided the book into six parts - Chest, Back, Legs, Arms, Shoulders/Neck, Abs – to cover all important muscle groups. Every muscle group contains 5 – 10 exercises, each with an illustration, safety tips and possible variations.

Before each segment you will find a short introduction about the muscle group and how to train it. Not all muscles are created equal and you have to know how to train every single one properly.

At last, I promise you that if you follow the advice in this book, you will increase both strength and size within a few weeks. Remember to always have fun and patience.

- Felix Harder

Chest

About the muscle:
Your chest is made up of two main muscles, the *Pectoralis Major* and the *Pectoralis Minor*.
The pectoralis major is a fan-shaped and thick muscle, located at the chest (anterior) of your body. It makes up the majority of the chest muscles in men and lies under the breast in women. The pectoralis minor is a thin, triangular muscle underneath the pectoralis major. In bodybuilding both are referred to as "pecs".

How to train chest:
Most bodybuilders agree that the chest is best trained using heavy pressing movements. This way, you will add mass and quickly increase the size of the muscle. Interestingly, the chest is only a medium sized muscle group, meaning you don't need too many sets to trigger muscle growth. As for reps, there is a one-number-fits-all solution. You should train between four and twelve repetitions. Otherwise, you risk shoulder problems.

Exercises that work the Pectoralis muscles include:

- Flat barbell bench press
- Incline barbell bench press
- Flat dumbbell bench press
- Dumbbell flys - Cable crossovers
- Pec deck machine
- Push-ups
- Dips

Bench Press

Main Muscle: Chest (Upper and lower pectorals)
Secondary Muscles: Shoulders, Triceps
Equipment: Barbell, Dumbbells (see variations)
Exercise Type: Compound
Force: Push

1. Setup
With your eyes under the bar, lie supine on the bench. Lift your chest and squeeze your shoulder blades. Your feet should be flat on the floor.

2. Grip
Place each pinky on the ring marks of your bar. Your grip should be medium-width grip (creating a 90-degree angle in the middle of the movement between your forearms and upper arms). Hold the bar in the base of your palm with straight wrists and a full grip.

3. Unrack
Take a big breath and dismount the barbell by straightening your arms. Move it over your shoulders, keeping your elbows locked.

4. Lower the bar
Lower the barbell to your chest. Your elbows should be at a 75° angle, while keeping your forearms vertical. Hold your breath at the bottom.

5. Press
Press the barbell upward until your arms are extended. The proper form is pressing the bar in a diagonal line from shoulders to chest and back up. This increases the distance, but prevents shoulder impingement. Your butt must also stay on the bench. Lock your elbows at the top and breathe.

Tips & Safety

- Don't let the bar drift too far forward. It should touch your middle chest and nowhere else.

- Never bounce the bar off your chest. You should always be in control of the weight.

- If you find yourself without a spotter, use a power rack. They have horizontal safety pins to catch the bar if you fail.

- Don't Bench Press using the "suicide grip" (thumbless grip). The barbell can slip out of your hands and drop on your chest.

Variations

Close Grip Bench Press:
This variation uses a narrow grip. You set up your flat bench like you do for the regular Bench Press, but this time, your grip is only about shoulder-width apart. Then lower the barbell to your chest. Close Grip Bench Press is harder than medium grip, because your (usually weaker) triceps work harder while your chest works less.

Wide Grip Bench Press:
This variation uses a wider than normal grip. You set up your flat bench like you do for the regular Bench Press. Your grip should be around three inches away from shoulder width for each hand. Then lower the barbell to your chest. Compared to a narrower grip, the wide grip works the pectoralis major more intensely and causes greater activity in the anterior deltoid.

Dumbbell Bench Press:

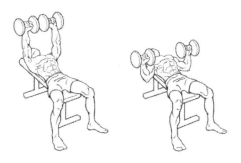

1. Setup

Sit down on the bench with each dumbbell resting on lower thigh.

2. Position

Kick the dumbbells to your shoulders and lie back. Position the weights to the sides of the chest with your elbows under them.

3. Execution

Press weights up to a lockout position. While pressing up, the dumbbells should follow an arch pattern, traveling inward and towards each other. At the top of the motion, both dumbbells should almost touch. Then, while keeping the elbows wide, lower the dumbbells to the sides of the chest. Repeat.

Incline Bench Press

Main Muscle: Upper Chest (Pectoralis Major, Clavicular)
Secondary Muscles: Shoulders, Triceps
Equipment: Barbell, Dumbbells (see variations)
Exercise Type: Compound
Force: Push

1. Setup
With your eyes under the bar, lie on an incline bench. Lift your chest and squeeze your shoulder blades. Your feet should be flat on the floor.

2. Grip
Place each pinky on the ring marks of your bar. Your grip should be medium-width grip (creating a 90-degree angle in the middle of the movement between your forearms and upper arms). Hold the bar in the base of your palm with straight wrists and a full grip.

3. Unrack
Take a big breath and dismount the barbell by straightening your arms. Move it over your shoulders, keeping your elbows locked.

4. Lower the bar
Lower the barbell to your upper chest. Hold your breath at the bottom.

5. Press
Press the barbell upward until your arms are extended. Squeeze your chest in the contracted position. Your butt must also stay on the bench. Lock your elbows at the top and breathe.

Tips & Safety

- Don't let the bar drift too far forward. It should touch your upper chest and nowhere else.

- Never bounce the bar off your chest. You should always be in control of the weight.

- If you find yourself without a spotter, use the smith machine. You will be able to lock in the bar at any height if you fail.

- Keep your shoulders and back flat on the bench and your abs drawn in throughout the exercise.

Variations

Wide & Close Grip: See normal Bench Press

Incline Dumbbell Bench Press:

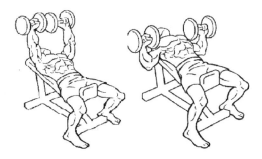

1. Setup
Set your bench at a 45-degree angle.

2. Position
Kick dumbbells to your shoulders and lie back. Bring both dumbbells to shoulder height (arms form a smaller than 90-degree angle).

3. Execution
Press weights up to a lockout position. While pressing up, the dumbbells should follow an arch pattern, traveling inward and towards each other. At the top of the motion, both dumbbells should almost touch. Then, while keeping the elbows wide, lower the dumbbells to the sides of the chest. Repeat.

Decline Bench Press

Main Muscle: Lower Chest (Pectoralis Major, Sternal)
Secondary Muscles: Shoulders, Triceps
Equipment: Barbell, Dumbbells (see variations)
Exercise Type: Compound
Force: Push

1. Setup
Lie on a decline bench. Your head should be lower than your feet (lock your feet under the pads at the front of the bench). Lift your chest and squeeze your shoulder blades.

2. Grip
Place each pinky on the ring marks of your bar. Your grip should be medium-width grip (creating a 90-degree angle in the middle of the movement between your forearms and upper arms). Hold the bar in the base of your palm with straight wrists and a full grip.

3. Unrack
Take a big breath and dismount the barbell by straightening your arms. Move it over your shoulders, keeping your elbows locked.

4. Lower the bar
Lower the barbell to the lower chest. Hold your breath at the bottom.

5. Press
Exhale and press the barbell upward until your arms are extended. Squeeze your chest in the contracted position. Lock your elbows at the top and breathe.

Tips & Safety

- Unlike the traditional Bench Press, the Decline Bench Press involves less rotation at the shoulders, thus preventing impingement.

- Due to the angle of the decline Bench Press, you will be able to lift more weight. This will stimulate the larger fibers of your muscles, which may have a small positive effect on your ability to build strength and size.

- Don't let the bar drift too far forward. It should touch your upper chest and nowhere else.

- Never bounce the bar off your chest. You should always be in control of the weight.

- Keep your shoulders and back flat on the bench and your abs drawn in throughout the exercise.

Variations

Wide & Close Grip: See normal Bench Press

Decline Dumbbell Bench Press:

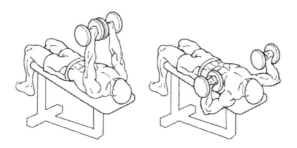

1. Setup
Sit down on decline bench with each dumbbell resting on lower thigh.

2. Position
Lie back with the dumbbells and position them to the sides of your chest. Position the weights to the sides of the chest with your elbows under them.

3. Execution
Press weights up to a lockout position. While pressing up, the dumbbells should follow an arch pattern, traveling inward and towards each other. At the top of the motion, both dumbbells should almost touch. Then, while keeping the elbows wide, lower the dumbbells to the sides of the chest. Repeat.

Dumbbell Flys

Muscle: Chest (Pectoralis Major, Sternal)
Secondary Muscle: Shoulders
Equipment: Dumbbells
Exercise Type: Isolation
Force: Push

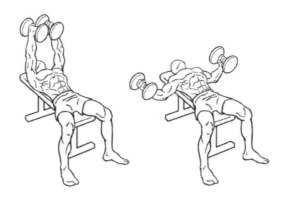

1. Setup
Sit down on flat bench with each dumbbell resting on lower thigh and the palms of your hands facing each other.

2. Position
Using your thighs to help raise the dumbbells, lie back and support them above your chest (arms should be fixed in slightly bent position, this prevents stress at the biceps tendon). Internally rotate shoulders so elbows point out to sides.

3. Execution
Breathe in as you lower your arms out at both sides in a wide arc until your chest muscles are stretched (without moving elbows). While breathing out, bring the dumbbells together using wide hugging motion and squeezing your chest muscles until they nearly touch. Repeat.

Tips & Safety

- Dumbbell Flys should be done slowly. The focus lies on the stretch and focusing of the pectoral muscles.

- If performed incorrectly or with too much weight, Dumbbell Flys can cause elbow and shoulder injuries. Stop if you feel any painful sensations or pinching.

- Don't let the dumbbells touch at the top of the exercise. This will keep the middle of your chest muscles under tension.

Incline Dumbbell Flys

Muscle: Upper Chest (Pectoralis Major, Clavicular)
Secondary Muscle: Shoulders
Equipment: Dumbbells
Exercise Type: Isolation
Force: Push

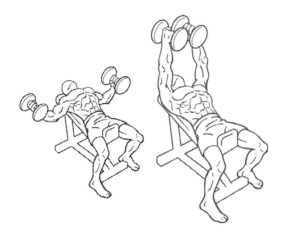

1. Setup
Sit down on an incline bench with each dumbbell resting on lower thigh and the palms of your hand facing each other.

2. Position
Lie back on the bench and extend your arms up, holding the dumbbells above your chest
(arms should be fixed in slightly bent position, this prevents stress at the biceps tendon). Internally rotate shoulders so elbows point out to sides.

3. Execution
Breathe in as you lower your arms out at both sides in a wide arc until your chest muscles are stretched (without moving elbows). While breathing out, bring the dumbbells together using wide hugging motion and squeezing your chest muscles until they nearly touch. Repeat.

Tips & Safety

- Incline Dumbbell Flys should be done slowly. The focus lies on the stretch and focusing of the pectoral muscles.

- If performed incorrectly or with too much weight, Dumbbell Flys can cause elbow and shoulder injuries. Stop if you feel any painful sensations or pinching.

- Don't let the dumbbells touch at the top of the exercise. This will keep the middle of your chest muscles under tension.

Incline Dumbbell Flys with a Twist:

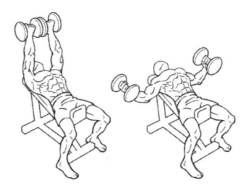

1. Setup
Sit down on an incline bench with each dumbbell resting on lower thigh and the palms of your hand facing each other.

2. Position
Lie back on the bench with your arms out to your sides, your elbows pointing down, and your palms facing up. Hold the dumbbells at about shoulder height.

3. Execution
While breathing out, focus on using your chest to bring up the dumbbells in a wide arc above the middle of your chest until they are directly above you. Turn your pinky fingers just before reaching the top so that your pinkies are facing each other and your palms are facing you.

Decline Dumbbell Flys

Muscle: Lower Chest (Pectoralis Major, Sternal)
Secondary Muscle: Shoulders
Equipment: Dumbbells
Exercise Type: Isolation
Force: Push

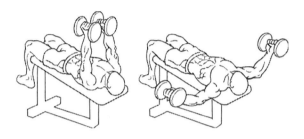

1. Setup
Sit down on a decline bench and secure your legs at the end of the bench. The dumbbells should be resting on the top of your thighs with the palms of your hand facing each other.

2. Position
Using your thighs to help raise the dumbbells, lie back and support them above your chest (arms should be fixed in slightly bent position, this prevents stress at the biceps tendon). Internally rotate shoulders so elbows point out to sides.

3. Execution
Breathe in as you lower your arms out at both sides in a wide arc until your chest muscles are stretched (without moving elbows). While breathing out, bring the dumbbells together using wide hugging motion and squeezing your chest muscles until they nearly touch. Repeat.

Butterfly / Pec Deck

Muscle: Chest (Pectoralis Major, Sternal)
Secondary Muscle: Shoulders
Equipment: Machine
Exercise Type: Isolation
Force: Pull

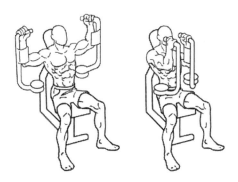

1. Setup
Sit on the machine with your back flat on the pad and your feet on the ground.

2. Position
Depending on the machine you are using, you should either place your arms on the pads with both elbows at a 90 degree angle (see above) or you grab the handles with your arms extended. You might need to adjust the seat, so your upper arms are positioned parallel to the floor.

3. Execution
Breathe out while slowly pushing both handles together. Squeeze your chest in the middle during this part of the motion and hold the contraction for a second. Then return back to the initial position as you inhale, until your chest muscles are fully stretched. Repeat.

Tips & Safety

- This exercise should only be performed with proper form and weight. When using too much weight, you will find your back lifting away from the pad and your head jutting forward.

- Watch your shoulders. Fly exercises can put strain on them. Immediately stop if you get any strange pains or tweaks in your shoulders.

- While a big range of motion is good, do not hyperextend the shoulders, as it can cause injury and/or long-term wear.

- Butterfly is a great exercise to do at the end of your chest day. It requires less stability and energy than heavy compound exercises such as bench press or incline bench press.

Bodyweight: Push-up

Muscle: Chest (Upper and lower pectorals)
Secondary Muscle: Shoulders, Triceps
Equipment: Body
Exercise Type: Compound
Force: Push

1. Position
Lie on the floor face down and place your hands slightly wider than shoulder width, while holding your torso up at arm's length. As you inhale, lower yourself downward (while keeping your body straight) until your chest almost touches the floor.

2. Execution
Now breathe out and push your upper body back up to the initial position while squeezing your chest. Pause at the top contracted position, then lower yourself downward again. Repeat for as many repetitions as needed.

Tips & Safety

- Try squeezing your core to avoid rounding your spine. This makes the push-up a full body exercise and reduces the risk of injury.

- A common mistake during push-ups is to flare the elbows wide. This can lead to rotator cuff and shoulder problems. It's better to pack your elbows in towards your sides, having less space between your armpits.

- Imagine pushing the floor away instead of pushing yourself off the ground. You will work more muscles making the push-up more of a full body exercise

Variations

Wide Push-ups:

Place your hands wider than shoulder width apart. This will work your chest more and your triceps less.

Triceps Push-ups:

Place your hands shoulder width apart (or less). This will work your triceps more and your chest less.

Exercise Ball Push-ups:

Place your feet on an exercise ball and hold your torso up with your hands slightly wider than shoulder width apart. Remember to keep your back straight and use an exercise ball that allows your body to be parallel to the ground when you have your arms fully extended.

Back

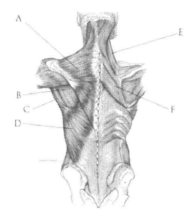

About the muscle:
The back, as a whole, is made up of several muscle groups: latissimus dorsi, erector spinae, rhomboids (major and minor), teres major, trapezius and posterior deltoids. Some of these muscles might also be considered parts of other muscle groups (e.g. shoulders). For training purposes, these muscles can be broken up into a three categories: upper back, lower back and trapezius.

How to train back:
Since the back is composed of so many individual muscles, it is a difficult body area to train.
In general, the best exercises to target the latissimus dorsi and teres major should allow you to bring your arms towards your sides. For example, lat pulldown and pull ups.
The best exercises for the middle and lower traps, along with the rhomboid major and minor, are exercises which make you squeeze your shoulder blades together, for example barbell rows and seated cable rows.

Deadlift

Main Muscle: Lower Back (Erector Spinae)
Secondary Muscles: Calves, Glutes, Hamstrings, Forearms, Lats, Quadriceps, Traps
Equipment: Barbell
Exercise Type: Compound
Force: Pull

1. Setup
Set up the barbell with appropriate weight. Don't lift too heavy if you have no experience with this exercise. It can be dangerous

2. Position
Bend your knees, while keeping your back as straight as possible. Bend forward and grasp the bar with an overhand grip. Your hands should be shoulder width apart. Some people have trouble holding on to the bar with this grip. You can also use the mixed grip (one palm facing up, one palm facing down).

3. Execution
While breathing out, push with your legs and get your torso to the upright position. At the top, stick your chest out and pull your shoulders back. Return to the initial position by bending at the knees and leaning the torso forward at the waist. Your back should be kept straight until the weights on the bar touch the floor.

Tips & Safety

- Focus more on your form and less on the weight. During your first workouts, practice the exercise with proper form and light weights. As your confidence grows, you can increase the weight.

- Don't look up while deadlifting. Your body should form a straight line from the top of your head to your lower back.

- Don't do this exercise if you have back issues, it will make them worse.

- Keep your back straight at all times. Lower back rounding or excess arching puts your spine at risk of serious injury.

Bent Over Barbell Row

Main Muscle: Middle Back
Secondary Muscles: Biceps, Lats, Shoulders
Equipment: Barbell
Exercise Type: Compound
Force: Pull

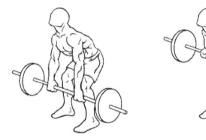

1. Setup
Set up the barbell with appropriate weight.

2. Position
Hold the barbell with your palms facing down and bend your knees slightly. While keeping the back straight, bring your torso forward. Legs and upper body should create a 100 – 120 degree angle (back almost parallel to the floor). The barbell should now hang directly in front of you.

3. Execution
While breathing out, pull up the barbell. Your elbows should be kept close to your body. Make sure to keep the torso stationary and squeeze your back muscles at the top. Inhale and then lower the barbell back to the starting position. Repeat.

Tips & Safety

- Make sure that you keep the head up during the entire exercise

- Don't do this exercise if you have back issues, it will make them worse.

- If your low back gets rounded due to tight hamstrings, either try bending your knees more or don't position the torso as low.

Bent Over Dumbbells Row (Single Arm):

1. Setup

Place one leg on top of the end of the bench; bend forward so your upper body is parallel to the floor. Position the hand of your supporting arm on the other end of the bench. Place your foot of the opposite leg slightly back to the side.

2. Position

Grasp the dumbbell with the other hand and hold the weight while keeping your lower back straight. Your palm should be facing towards your torso.

3. Execution

Breathe out and pull the weight straight up to the side of your chest until it touches your ribs or until your upper arm is just beyond horizontal. Make sure to keep your torso stationary and the upper arm close to your side. Squeeze your back muscles at the top. While breathing in, lower the dumbbell straight down to the starting position. Repeat and don't forget to switch sides.

Tips & Safety

- The exercise should be performed with the back muscles and not the arms. Therefore, don't try to pull the weight up using the forearms.

- You can allow the scapula to move but don't rotate torso trying to "throw" the weight up.

- When using heavier weight, position your leg on a lower bench to allow the dumbbell to touch the floor.

Cable Row

Main Muscle: Upper Back (Trapezius, Rhomboids)
Secondary Muscles: Biceps, Lats, Shoulders
Equipment: Barbell
Exercise Type: Compound
Force: Pull

1. Setup
Sit down on a low pulley row machine with a V-bar.

2. Position
Position your feet on the front platform. Sit slightly forward on seat or bench and grab the V-bar. Your knees should be slightly bent and your back straight.

3. Execution
Pull back until your torso is at a 90-degree angle from your legs (your arms should be extended at this point). Breathe in and pull the handles back towards your torso. Your arms should be close to your torso until the handle touches your abs. Pull your shoulders back and push chest forward while arching your back. Slowly go back to the starting position while breathing in. Repeat.

Tips & Safety

- Your lower back will need time to adapt to the exercise. Start using light weight and add additional weight gradually.

- Don't pause at bottom of the lift. You should feel a mild stretch during the entire exercise.

- Remember to squeeze your shoulder blades together as you row.

T-Bar Row

Main Muscle: Middle Back (Trapezius, erector spinae)
Secondary Muscles: Biceps
Equipment: Machine, Barbell
Exercise Type: Compound
Force: Pull

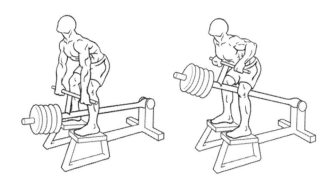

1. Setup
Load the machine with the desired weight or use a barbell and position it in in a corner to keep it from moving.

2. Position
Stand over the bar and grab the handle. If you are using a free barbell, place a Double D row handle around it next to the collar. Stand up using your hips and legs. Your legs should be in a wide stance with your chest up, your hips back and your arms extended.

3. Execution
While retracting your shoulder blades and flexing the elbows, pull up the weight to your upper abdomen. This should be done slowly without jerking. Then lower the weight to the original position. Repeat

Tips & Safety

- This exercise should be done early in your workout to make sure you have enough energy.

- Finish the movement by pulling the weight to your chest.

- The row should be finished by bringing your shoulder blades together.

- Keep your back straight and your body aligned.

Lat Pulldown

Main Muscle: Back (latissimus dorsi)
Secondary Muscles: Biceps, Middle Back, Shoulders
Equipment: Cable
Exercise Type: Compound
Force: Pull

1. Setup
Set up the pull-down machine with a wide bar attached to the cable. When sitting down, make sure to adjust the knee-pad according to your height.

2. Position
Using a wide grip, grab the bar with your palms facing forward. With your arms extended and holding the bar, lean back around 30 degrees and stick your chest out.

3. Execution
While breathing out, pull down the bar until it touches your upper chest. The pulling is done primarily with your back muscles rather than your biceps. Draw your shoulders and upper arms down and back while bringing down the weight. Keep your upper body stable during the exercise. Pause for a moment and then return the bar to the original position. Repeat

Tips & Safety

- Use slow and controlled movements and make sure you do not cheat by swinging your back.

- Many bodybuilders avoid pulling down the weight behind the neck, as it can be hard on the rotator cuff due to the hyperextension created.

- Do not hunch over or drop your shoulders.

Bodyweight: Pull-up

Muscle: Back (latissimus dorsi)
Secondary Muscle: Biceps
Equipment: Body
Exercise Type: Compound
Force: Pull

1. Position

Using a wider than shoulder width grip, grab the pull-up bar with the palms facing forward.
With your arms extended and holding the bar, bring back your torso around 30 degrees and stick your chest out.

2. Execution

While breathing out, pull your upper body up until it touches your chest by drawing the shoulders and the upper arms down and back. The pulling is done primarily with your back muscles rather than your biceps. Draw your shoulders and upper arms down and back while raising your torso. Pause for a moment and then return to the original position. Repeat.

Tips & Safety

- Your forearms should do no other work other than hold the bar.

- If you don't have enough strength to perform this exercise, ask a spotter to hold your legs or use a chin assist machine

- By using a weight belt, you can increase the difficulty

Variations

Hand placement:
- Pronated grip (palms face away from you)
- Supinated grip (palms facing you)
- Mixed grip (one palm facing away, 1 palm facing you)

Other:

- Climber pull-up: Pull yourself up towards one hand.

- Alternating Climber pull-up: Pull yourself up towards one hand. Stay at the position, and move your body towards the other hand and lower yourself.

- Uneven pull-up: Hang a towel over the bar and grab it with one hand. Grab the bar with the other hand. Pull yourself up until your chin is just over the bar.

Legs

Muscles of the Lower Extremity

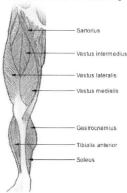

Sartorius

Vastus intermedius

Vastus lateralis

Vastus medialis

Gastrocnemius

Tibialis anterior

Soleus

About the muscle:
Just as the back, your legs are made up of many individual muscles: Hamstrings (form the back of the thigh), Adductors (a.k.a, the inner thigh muscles), Quadriceps (at the front of your thigh), Gastrocnemius (uppermost of your two calf muscles), Soleus (underneath the gastrocnemius), and Tibialis anterior (strip of muscle that makes up your shin).

How to train legs:
If you want to build big legs, you will need to push your muscles to, or almost to, failure and then them rest and grow. Depending on your split, you will want to train 2-4 sets with 6-12 repetitions with heavy enough weights. Some bodybuilders dedicate an entire day just to their leg training.

Barbell Squat

Main Muscle: Quadriceps
Secondary Muscles: Calves, Glutes, Hamstrings, Lower Back
Equipment: Barbell
Exercise Type: Compound
Force: Push

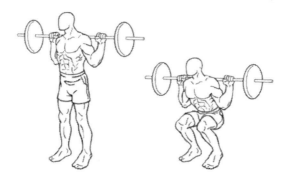

1. Setup
Load the bar with the desired weight and set it on a rack to just below shoulder level.

2. Position
Step under the bar and place it slightly below the neck across the back of your shoulders. Grab the bar using a slightly wider than shoulder width grip. Lift the bar off the rack by pushing with your legs and then straightening your torso. Place your legs in a medium stance (feet shoulder width apart); your toes should be slightly pointed out.

3. Execution
Bend your knees and slowly lower the bar. While inhaling, descend until your thighs are just past parallel to the floor. Then raise the bar as you exhale. Imagine pushing the floor with the heel of your foot as you straighten your legs. Repeat.

Tips & Safety

- Keep your head facing forward and your back straight at all times.

- Watch out for equal distribution of weight throughout your forefoot and heel.

- If you have back issues, substitute the exercise with the dumbbell squat variation.

Dumbbell Squat to Bench:

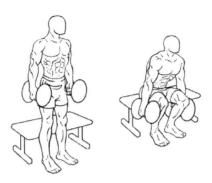

1. Setup
Find a bench appropriate in size. It should be just lower than your knees.

2. Position
Stand in front of the bench and hold the dumbbells at your sides with your feet shoulder width apart.

3. Execution
While breathing in, slowly bend forward at the knees. Allow your hips to bend back as if you were sitting down. Stop when your butt touches the bench, but don't sit down. While exhaling, return to the original position by pressing upwards and extending your legs. Maintain a straight back and an equal distribution of weight on your forefoot and heel. Repeat.

Leg Press

Main Muscle: Quadriceps
Secondary Muscles: Calves, Glutes, Hamstrings
Equipment: Machine
Exercise Type: Compound
Force: Push

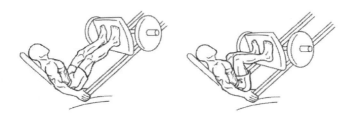

1. Setup

Load the machine with the desired weight.

2. Position

Sit down on the machine and place your legs on the platform in front of you. Your feet should be about shoulder width apart. Release the dock lever, grasp the handles to your sides and press the platform all the way up until your legs are fully extended.

3. Execution

While inhaling, lower the platform until your upper and lower legs create a 90-degree angle.
Then, push back the platform to the original position, using the heels of your feet and your quadriceps. Exhale during this movement. Repeat.

Tips & Safety

- Don't lock your knees at the top.

- You should keep your knees pointed in the same direction as your feet.

- Placing your feet slightly higher on the platform will emphasize the Gluteus Maximus. Placing them lower emphasizes Quadriceps

Dumbbell Lunges

Main Muscle: Quadriceps
Secondary Muscles: Calves, Glutes, Hamstrings
Equipment: Dumbbell
Exercise Type: Compound
Force: Push

 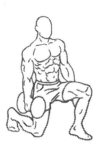

1. Position
Stand with two dumbbells in your hands as seen in the picture.

2. Execution
Step forward with one leg. Land first on your heel, then forefoot. Lower your body by flexing the hip and knee of the front leg until the knee of the rear leg almost touches the floor. While exhaling, push up and go back to the original position. Use mainly the heel for this movement. Repeat by alternating lunge with opposite legs.

Tips & Safety

- Don't allow the knee of your front leg to go beyond your toes as you lower your body. This will stress your knee joint.

- Remember to keep your front shin perpendicular to the ground.

- Avoid this exercise if you have balance problems.

Variations

Static Lunges: Using only one leg, go up and down from the starting position. Later switch the leg and do the same.

Walking Lunges: Instead of returning to the starting position, walk across the room in a lunging fashion.

Using a Barbell: This variation should be used by experienced athletes with no balance issues.

Leg Extensions

Main Muscle: Quadriceps
Equipment: Machine
Exercise Type: Isolation
Force: Push

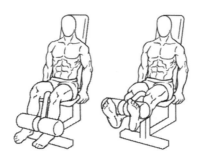

1. Setup
Choose your weight on the leg extension machine.

2. Position
Sit down and position your legs under the pad with your feet pointed forward. The pad should sit just on top of your lower leg. Your knee articulation should be positioned at the same axis as lever fulcrum. Grab the side bars with your hands.

3. Execution
While exhaling, extend your legs to the maximum, using only your quadriceps. Your upper body should remain stationary. Pause a second at the top. While inhaling, slowly lower the weight back to the starting position. Repeat.

Tips & Safety

- When in the starting position, make sure that your lower and upper leg form a 90-degree angle.

- Don't swing your legs during the exercise.

Variation

- You can use one leg at a time instead of both at once.

Lying Leg Curls

Main Muscle: Hamstrings
Equipment: Machine
Exercise Type: Isolation
Force: Pull

1. Setup
Adjust the machine lever to fit your height. Place the pad just a few inches under your calves.

2. Position
Lie down on the bench and grab the side handles of the machine. Your legs should be fully stretched.
Position your toes straight.

3. Execution
While exhaling and without lifting the upper legs from the pad, curl your legs up as far as possible. Hold
it for a second, once you hit the fully contracted position. Then, while inhaling,
bring your legs back to the starting position. Repeat.

Tips & Safety

- Try to find a leg curl machine that is angled (as opposed to flat). This position is more favorable for hamstrings recruitment.

- Advanced trainees can raise their upper body off the pad a little bit. It will force you to focus even more on your hamstrings.

Variation

- The exercise can also be performed as a seated leg curl or with a dumbbell held in between your feet (a partner will need to place it properly).

Seated Calf Raises

Main Muscle: Calves
Equipment: Machine
Exercise Type: Isolation
Force: Push

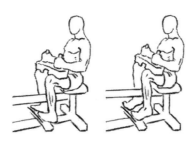

1. Setup
Load the machine with desired weight.

2. Position
Sit down and position your toes on the lower portion of the platform. You heels should be hanging off. Place your thighs under the lever pad and your hands on top of the lever pad as seen in the picture.

3. Execution
Push your heels up and lift the lever slightly. While inhaling, slowly lower your heels by bending at the ankles. Continue this movement until your calves are fully stretched. While exhaling, raise the heels by extending your ankles as high as possible. Hold the contraction for a second and repeat.

Tips & Safety

- Push your heels up as far as possible and let the calves stretch out as far as possible to use a full range of motion.

- For extra intensity, pause and count to three at the top of the movement.

- Change the position of your toes (outwards / inwards) to work your calves at differing angles.

Variation

- This exercise can be done standing up as well. Standing Calf Raises will target the gastrocs more than the soleus (a different part of the calf).

Arms

Muscles of the Upper Extremity

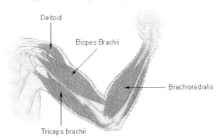

About the muscle:
Both our arms are composed of different muscles. The most important arm muscles in bodybuilding
are:
- Biceps (formally known as the biceps brachii muscle), which rests on top of the humerus bone. It
flexes the elbow and rotates the forearm.
- Triceps (formally known as the triceps brachii muscle), which helps straighten the arm.
- Brachioradialis, which rotates the forearm and also flexes it at the elbow.

How to train arms:
In order to get big arms, you will need to do both compound and isolation exercises. The compound
movements are needed to increase strength, but by themselves won't get you significantly bigger arms.
To target specific arm muscles you will also have to do some isolation exercises such as the ones
below.

Barbell Curl

Main Muscle: Biceps
Secondary Muscles: Forearms
Equipment: Barbell
Exercise Type: Isolation
Force: Pull

1. Setup
Load the bar with desired weight.

2. Position
With you back straight, hold the barbell at a shoulder-width grip (palms facing forward). Keep your elbows close to the torso.

3. Execution
While exhaling, curl the barbell forward while contracting the biceps. Don't move your upper arms. Raise the bar until it is at shoulder level and your biceps are fully contracted. Squeeze your biceps at the top. While inhaling, slowly bring the bar back to the original position. Repeat.

Tips & Safety

- Don't swing the bar or your body.

- Stay in control of the weight at all times. Don't let it drop quickly.

Variation

- You can also perform this exercise using an E-Z bar. Some people prefer the E-Z bar due to its ergonomic grip.

Alternating Dumbbell Curls

Main Muscle: Biceps
Secondary Muscles: Forearms
Equipment: Dumbbell
Exercise Type: Isolation
Force: Pull

1. Position

Stand with your feet shoulder width apart and a dumbbell in each hand. Your knees should be slightly bent and your elbows close to the torso (palms facing your thighs).

2. Execution

While exhaling, curl the right dumbbell as you rotate the palm of your hand until it is facing forward. While keeping your elbows locked, continue to lift your arm to your chest until your forearm touches your biceps. Squeeze the biceps at the top. While inhaling, slowly bring the dumbbell back to the initial position. Repeat the movement with the other hand.

Tips & Safety

- Keep your elbows locked in throughout the exercise.

- Twist back the palms to the original position as you come down.

- Keeping your knees slightly bent will prevent you from swinging your torso.

Variation

- You can perform this exercise using both arms at the same time, sitting down (with or without back support), or without turning the palms.

Alternating Hammer Curls

Main Muscle: Biceps
Equipment: Dumbbell
Exercise Type: Isolation
Force: Pull

1. Position
Stand with your feet shoulder width apart and a dumbbell in each hand. Your knees should be slightly bent and your elbows close to the torso (palms facing each other).

2. Execution
While exhaling, curl the right dumbbell and lift your arm to your chest until your forearm touches your biceps. Squeeze the biceps at the top. While inhaling, slowly bring the dumbbell back to the initial position. Repeat the movement with the other hand.

Tips & Safety

- Do not turn your wrists during the exercise.

- Keep your elbows locked in throughout the exercise.

- Keeping your knees slightly bent will prevent you from swinging your torso.

Variation

- You can perform this exercise using both arms at the same time, sitting down (with or without back support).

Bodyweight: Chin Up

Main Muscle: Biceps
Secondary Muscles: Forearms, Lats, Middle Back
Equipment: Body
Exercise Type: Compound
Force: Pull

1. Position
Using a closer than shoulder width grip, grab the pull-up bar with the palms facing inward.
With your arms extended and holding the bar, bring back your torso around 30 degrees and stick your chest out.

2. Execution
While breathing out, pull your upper body up until your head is around the level of the pull-up bar. The pulling is done primarily with your biceps. Keep your elbows close to your body. Pause for a moment and then return to the original position. Repeat.

Tips & Safety

- Your forearms should do no other work other than hold the bar.

- If you don't have enough strength to perform this exercise, ask a spotter to hold your legs or use a chin assist machine.

- By using a weight belt, you can increase the difficulty.

Variations

Hand placement:
- Pronated grip (palms face away from you).
- Supinated grip (palms facing you).
- Mixed grip (one palm facing away, 1 palm facing you).

Lying Triceps Press / Skullcrusher

Main Muscle: Triceps
Secondary Muscles: Forearms
Equipment: Barbell, E-Z Curl Bar
Exercise Type: Isolation
Force: Push

1. Setup
Lie on a flat bench and place a straight bar (or an E-Z bar) behind your head.

2. Position
With your feet on the floor, grab the bar, using a shoulder width overhand (pronated) grip. Keep your elbows tucked in.

3. Execution
Raise the bar in front of you at arm's length. While inhaling, lower the bar until it almost touches your forehead. Keep your upper arms and elbows stationary. While exhaling, use your triceps to bring the weight back. Repeat.

Tips & Safety

- Don't use too much weight the first time you do this exercise.

- If you have elbow problems you may need to look for a substitute.

Variations

- You can use an incline bench instead of a flat bench.

- You can also use dumbbells instead of a barbell. Your palms should be facing each other.

Triceps Pushdown

Main Muscle: Triceps
Equipment: Cable
Exercise Type: Isolation
Force: Push

1. Setup
Set up the high pulley with a straight bar attached to the cable.

2. Position
Grab the bar with an overhand grip (palms facing down) at shoulder width. Stand upright with your back straight, while leaning slightly forward. Keep your upper arms close to your body.

3. Execution
While exhaling, bring the bar down until your arms are fully extended or it touches your thighs. This movement is performed using only your triceps. Keep your upper arms stationary next and don't swing your body. Hold the contracted position, then bring the bar slowly up to the initial point. Inhale as you perform this step. Repeat.

Tips & Safety

- You should stay close to cable to provide resistance at the top of the motion.

- Avoid this exercise if you have elbow problems or if you develop elbow soreness over time.

Variations

- An E-Z bar attachment or a V-angled bar will allow your thumb to be higher than the small finger, thus working different parts of your triceps.

- You can also attach a rope to the pulley or use a reverse grip.

Bodyweight: Triceps Dip

Main Muscle: Triceps
Secondary Muscles: Chest, Shoulders
Equipment: Body
Exercise Type: Compound
Force: Push

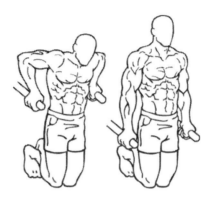

1. Position

With your arms almost locked, hold your body above the bars.

2. Execution

While inhaling, slowly lower yourself downward until there is a 90 degree angle formed between the upper arm and forearm. Your upper body should remain upright while keeping your elbows close to your body. While exhaling, push your body back to the original position using your triceps. Repeat.

Tips & Safety

- If you don't have enough strength to perform this exercise, ask a spotter to hold your legs or use a dip assist machine.

- By using a weight belt, you can increase the difficulty.

Variations

- Dips can be done as either a triceps or a chest exercise. The more you lean forward while performing the exercise, the more your chest will be involved.

Shoulders / Neck

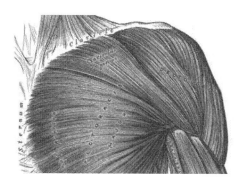

About the muscle:
The shoulders are a complex system of muscles responsible for a great amount of movement. In bodybuilding, you will focus on two layers of muscles called the deltoid and the rotator cuff. The deltoid is composed of the anterior head, the middle head and the posterior head. Usually all three work together, for example, when you take your arm overhead.
Underneath this first layer you find the rotator cuff, which is made up of four more muscles (infraspinatus, teres minor, supraspinatus and subscapularis). These muscles help stabilize and rotate the arm.

How to train shoulders:
You don't need to do hundreds of isolation exercises for your shoulders. They get a workout doing big, compound movements like the overhead press and even the bench press. Remember to train heavy and hard, since your muscles won't grow unless they need to.

Seated Barbell Military Press / Shoulder Press

Main Muscle: Shoulders
Secondary Muscles: Triceps
Equipment: Barbell
Exercise Type: Compound
Force: Push

1. Setup
Sit on a Military Press Bench with the bar in front of you on the rack.

2. Position
Carefully pick up the bar with a slightly wider than shoulder width grip (palms facing forward). Lift it over your head by extending your arms. Stop at about shoulder level (the bar should be slightly in front of your head).

3. Execution
While inhaling, lower the bar down to your upper chest. Then lift it back up to the original position. Exhale while doing this movement.

Tips & Safety

- Make sure to set the barbell slightly below shoulder height so it can be more easily unracked.

- Your range of motion will be compromised if your grip is too wide.

- Always keep your back straight to not lose control of the weight.

Variation

- Military Press can also be performed standing up, however. if you have lower back problems, you should use the seated variety.

- You can lower the bar behind the neck, but this may cause shoulder problems, as it can be hard on the rotator cuff due to the hyperextension created.

Dumbbell Shoulder Press:

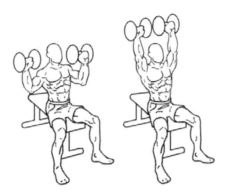

1. Setup
Sit on a flat bench (with back support).

2. Position
Place the dumbbells on your thighs. Lift up the dumbbells to shoulder height using your thighs to help propel them up into position (your palms should be facing forward).

3. Execution
While exhaling, push up both dumbbells until they almost touch at the top. Hold the contracted position for a second, then slowly lower the weights back down to the original position while inhaling.

Side Lateral Raise

Main Muscle: Shoulders
Equipment: Dumbbell
Exercise Type: Isolation
Force: Push

1. Position

Stand up straight with the dumbbells in your hands (palms facing you) and your arms extended.

2. Execution

While exhaling and keeping your upper body stationary, lift both dumbbells to your side until your arms are parallel to the floor. There should be a slight bend on the elbow. Pause for a second at the top. Then, lower the dumbbells back down to the initial position as you inhale.

Tips & Safety

- This exercise can cause shoulder problems if done wrong. By leaning forward just a bit at the waist, you position the medial deltoid in a more direct line of force opposing gravity. This now allows you to make the exercise safe for your shoulders.

Variations

- This exercise can also be performed sitting down or with one arm at a time.

Barbell Front Raise

Main Muscle: Shoulders
Equipment: Dumbbell
Exercise Type: Isolation
Force: Pull

1. Setup
Load a straight or E-Z bar with the weight you want to use.

2. Position
Grasp the bar using an overhand grip (palms facing down). Your hands should be around shoulder width apart and your arms extended.

3. Execution
While exhaling, slowly raise the barbell up to shoulder height. After holding the top contracted position, slowly lower the barbell back to the original position as you inhale.
Repeat.

Tips & Safety

- Focus on strict technique to isolate the front deltoids.

- Don't let the barbell touch your thighs during the set, and don't raise it above shoulder level.

- Keep your back straight and your mid-section tight at all times.

Variations

- You can change the grip (palms facing up) or use dumbbells instead.

Dumbbell Upright Row

Main Muscle: Traps
Secondary Muscle: Shoulders, Biceps, Upper Back
Equipment: Dumbbell
Exercise Type: Compound
Force: Pull

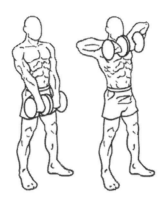

1. Position
Stand up straight with the dumbbells in your hands (palms forward) and your arms extended. The dumbbells should be slightly less than shoulder width apart. Keep your back straight and a slight bend at the elbows.

2. Execution
While exhaling, lift the dumbbells, using only your side shoulders until they nearly touch your chin. They should remain close to your body throughout the motion. Pause for a second at the top and then slowly lower the dumbbells back down. Inhale as you lower the dumbbells. Repeat.

Tips & Safety

- The elbows should drive the motion. While lifting the dumbbells, your elbows should always be higher than the forearms.

- Don't swing or jerk the dumbbells.

- Too much weight can easily lead to bad form in this exercise.

Variations

- This exercise can also be performed using a barbell or a straight bar attached to a low pulley.

Dumbbell Shrug

Main Muscle: Traps
Equipment: Cable
Exercise Type: Isolation
Force: Pull

1. Position
Stand up straight with the dumbbells in your hands (palms facing each other) and your arms extended. Keep your back straight and a slight bend at the elbows.

2. Execution
While exhaling, raise your shoulders (shrug) as far as you can. Pause for a second at the top and then slowly lower your shoulders back down while inhaling. Repeat.

Tips & Safety

- Your feet should be planted firmly on the floor throughout the exercise. You might also want to try bending your knees slightly.

- If you have difficulty holding the weight, use wrist wraps for better grip.

- Concentrate on only shrugging at the shoulder joint to complete each repetition. Don't use your arms in any way.

Variations

- You can also rotate your shoulders in a semi-circular motion from front to back.

- You can also use a barbell or the smith machine.

Cable Front Raise

Main Muscle: Shoulders
Equipment: Cable
Exercise Type: Isolation
Force: Push

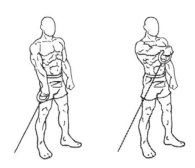

1. Setup
Attach a handle to the cable pulley at the lowest setting.

2. Position
Stand straight with your back facing the tower. The handle should be in your left hand (palms facing your thighs) in front of your left thigh and your arm extended.

3. Execution
While exhaling, lift the left handle in front of you until your arm is just above your shoulder and past parallel to the floor. Keep your body stationary and a slight bend in your elbow during this movement. After a short pause, slowly lower the weight to the initial position, while inhaling. Repeat.

Tips & Safety

- Don't swing the weight. Bending your knees slightly might help avoid cheating.

- Your wrists should remain straight with your palms facing down.

- Focus on only moving at the shoulder joint to perform the exercise.

Variations

- You can change the grip (palms facing up) or use dumbbells instead.

Abs

Muscles of the Trunk

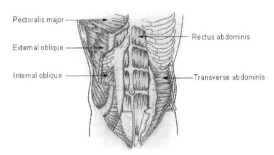

About the muscle:
The abdominal muscles are comprised of three layers: the deep-, the intermediate- and the superficial layer. The superficial layer is what we usually talk about, when referring to a six-pack. It is made up of the external oblique (runs from the ribcage down to your hips) and the rectus abdominus (the muscle "packs" in the six-pack).

How to train Abs:
If you are already doing compound exercises such as the deadlift, all you need is 10-15 minutes at the end of your workout routine. An entire ab-day is useless in my opinion, but some bodybuilders disagree. Never do abs first, because you will lack core strength in later compound exercises. Remember to hit your abs from different angles and try out new exercises every once in a while.

Ab Crunch

Main Muscle: Abdominals
Equipment: Body
Exercise Type: Isolation
Force: Pull

1. Position
Lie flat on your back with your feet resting on a bench with your knees bent at a 90-degree angle, or flat on the ground.

2. Execution
With hands lightly on either side of your head or neck, begin to roll your shoulders off the floor. They should come up off the floor only about 4 inches, while your lower back should remain on the floor. At the top of the motion, contract your abdominals hard and maintain the contraction for a second. Then, slowly lower to the original motion.

Tips & Safety

- Keep your lower back against the floor and your hips straight during the exercise.

- Focus on slow, controlled movement. Don't cheat yourself by swinging your upper body.

Variations

- There are hundreds of variations for the ab crunch. You can perform the exercise on top of an exercise ball or on a decline bench or with weights.

Twisting Crunch / Cross Body Crunch

Main Muscle: Abdominals
Equipment: Body
Exercise Type: Isolation
Force: Pull

1. Position
Lie flat on a mat. Position your hands behind head or neck.

2. Execution
Flex and twist your waist to raise your upper torso while bringing your left knee in toward your left shoulder at the same time. Reach with your elbow and try to touch your knee. Return until the backs of your shoulders touches the mat. Repeat on opposite side, alternating twists.

Tips & Safety

- While you cannot add weight to this exercise, you can concentrate on slow speed and perfect execution.

- Don't cheat yourself by jerking your upper body.

Variations

- You can also do all of your reps for one side and then switch to the other side.

Leg Raise

Main Muscle: Abdominals
Equipment: Body
Exercise Type: Isolation
Force: Pull

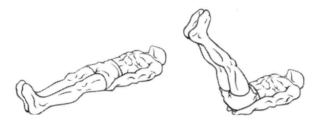

1. Position
Lie flat on a mat. Position your hands under your glutes with your palms down.

2. Execution
While exhaling and keeping your legs as straight as possible, raise your legs until they create a 90-degree angle with the floor. Hold the contraction at the top for a second. While inhaling, slowly lower your legs back down to the original position.

Tips & Safety

- Keep your lower back against the floor and your hips straight during the exercise.

- Focus on slow, controlled movement. Don't cheat yourself by swinging your legs.

Variations

- You can also perform this exercise on a bench with your legs hanging off.

- Advanced lifters can also add weight by holding a dumbbell in between their feet.

Side Plank Exercise

Main Muscle: Obliques
Secondary Muscle. Shoulders
Equipment: Body

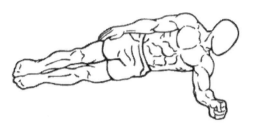

1. Position
Lie on one side and support your body between your forearm and knee to your feet.

2. Execution
While drawing your abs in, slowly raise your body so you are balanced on your feet and your forearm (see picture). Hold this position for about 30 - 60 seconds and slowly return back to the initial position. Switch sides and repeat.

Tips & Safety

- Do not let your waist sag. You will need to keep your upper body and legs straight while holding your own weight on your forearm.

- Gradually increase the time you hold the top position in future workout routines.

Ab Rollout

Main Muscle: Abdominals
Secondary Muscles: Deltoids, Lats, Lower Back
Equipment: Barbell
Exercise Type: Compound
Force: Pull

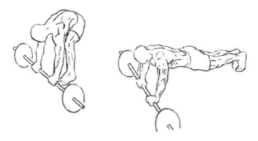

1. Position
Go into a pushup position and grab on to a barbell loaded with 5-10 lbs. on each side.

2. Execution
While exhaling, lift your hips and roll the barbell towards your feet. Remember to keep a slight arch on your back. Your arms should remain perpendicular to the floor throughout the movement. Otherwise you will work out your back and shoulders more than the abs. Hold the contraction at the top for a second, then start to roll the barbell back and forward to the initial position slowly as you inhale.

Tips & Safety

- This exercise should not be done if you have back problems or difficulties maintaining stability.

- Keep your arms straight throughout the exercise.

Variations

- For less advanced athletes, this exercise can also be done on your knees.

Other Books By Felix Harder

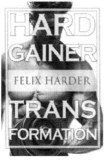  

Click On The Cover To Go To The Book

Made in the USA
Lexington, KY
12 March 2018